Victorian
DECORATIVE
BORDERS
and DESIGNS

CHRISTOPHER DRESSER
AND OTHERS

DOVER PUBLICATIONS, INC.
MINEOLA, NEW YORK

Copyright

Copyright © 2008 by Dover Publications, Inc.
All rights reserved.

Bibliographical Note

This Dover edition, first published in 2008, is a new selection of plates from *Studies in Design,* by Christopher Dresser, originally published by Cassell, Petter and Galpin, London, in 1876 (pages 1-47), and *Album du Peintre en Bâtiment,* by N. Glaise, originally published by Ducher et Cie, Paris, in 1875 (pages 48-75).

DOVER *Pictorial Archive* SERIES

This book belongs to the Dover Pictorial Archive Series. You may use the designs and illustrations for graphics and crafts applications, free and without special permission, provided that you include no more than ten in the same publication or project. (For permission for additional use, please write to Permissions Department, Dover Publications, Inc., 31 East 2nd Street, Mineola, N.Y. 11501.)

However, republication or reproduction of any illustration by any other graphic service, whether it be in a book or in any other design resource, is strictly prohibited.

Library of Congress Cataloging-in-Publication Data

Victorian decorative borders and designs / Christopher Dresser and others.
     p. cm. — (Dover pictorial archive series)
   "This Dover edition, first published in 2008, is a new selection of plates from Studies in design, by Christopher Dresser, originally published by Cassell, Petter and Galpin, London, in 1876, and Album du peintre en bâtiment, by N. Glaise, originally published by Ducher et Cie, Paris, in 1875."
  ISBN-13: 978-0-486-46135-9
  ISBN-10: 0-486-46135-1
  1. Decoration and ornament—Victorian style. 2. Borders, Ornamental (Decorative arts) 3. Interior walls—Decoration. 4. Pattern books. I. Dresser, Christopher. Studies in design. Selections. II. Glaise, N. Album du peintre en bâtiment. Selections.

NK1530.V49 2008
745.409'034—dc22

                       2007049436

Manufactured in the United States of America
Dover Publications, Inc., 31 East 2nd Street, Mineola, N.Y. 11501

Note

This exquisite collection features over 160 Victorian designs selected from two rare, late-nineteenth-century portfolios: *Studies in Design,* by renowned artist Christopher Dresser and *Album du Peintre en Bâtiment,* a source of decorative elements selected by N. Glaise. The illustrations in this book were intended to be useful to manufacturers of wall panels, curtains, relief ornaments, borders, lace, carpets, carved stonework, and more.

Christopher Dresser (1834–1904) was one of the leading industrial designers of the Victorian era. At the age of thirteen, Dresser attended the Government School of Design at Somerset House, in London, where he studied botany and design. This is where he met his mentor, Owen Jones, who became so impressed with Dresser's floral designs that he asked him to contribute a plate of plant forms to *The Grammar of Ornament* (available as a Dover reprint). Dresser is best known for creating simple, affordable, functional items to beautify the home, such as wallpaper, textiles, ceramics, glassware, furniture and metalware. He was one of the first designers to take full advantage of modern manufacturing methods, enabling him to mass produce a wide range of merchandise, as opposed to only handcrafted pieces. Many of his designs were influenced by his knowledge of botany and the Japanese style of ornamentation. *Studies in Design* was created "to bring about a better style of decoration for our houses," and is considered to be Dresser's masterpiece.

Christopher Dresser's artwork can be found between pages 1 and 47. The designs from pages 48 to 75 were selected from a variety of different sources by N. Glaise and are also excellent examples of Victorian design.

4

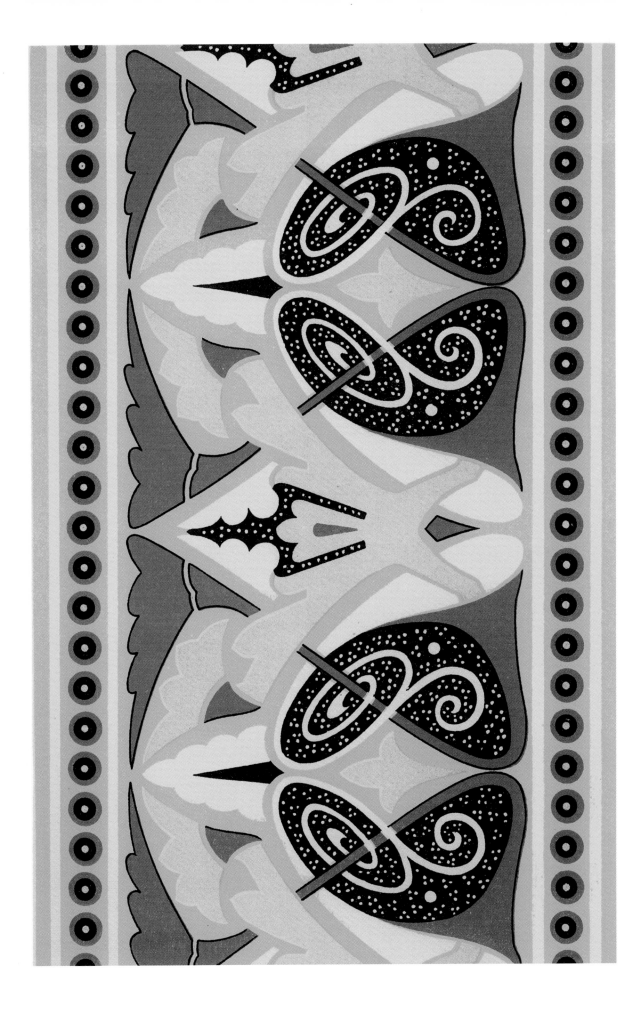

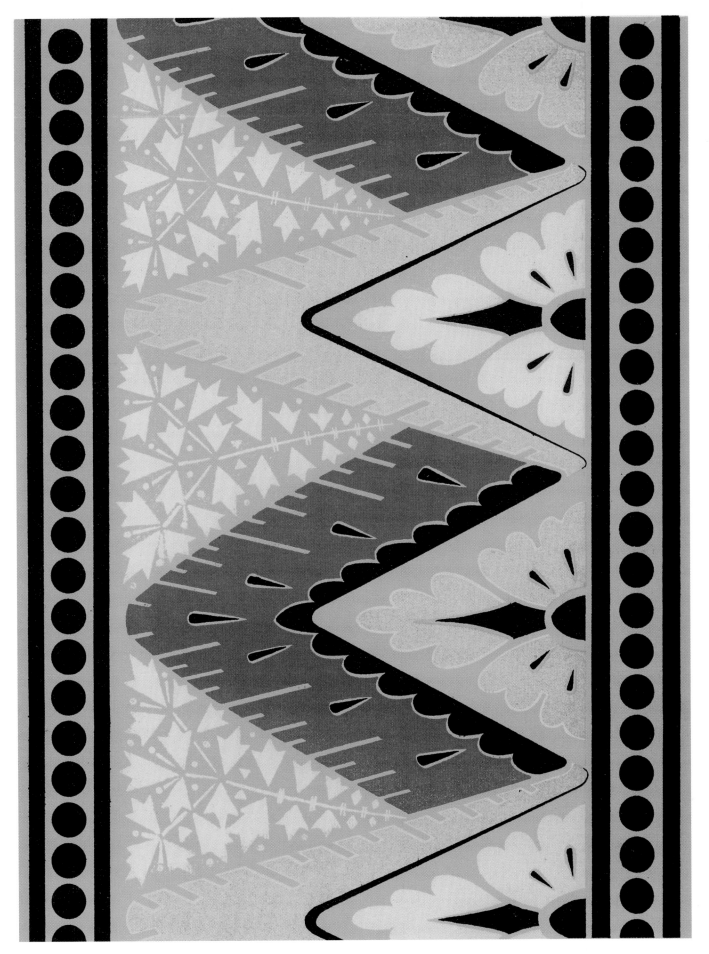

9

12

14

15

16

20

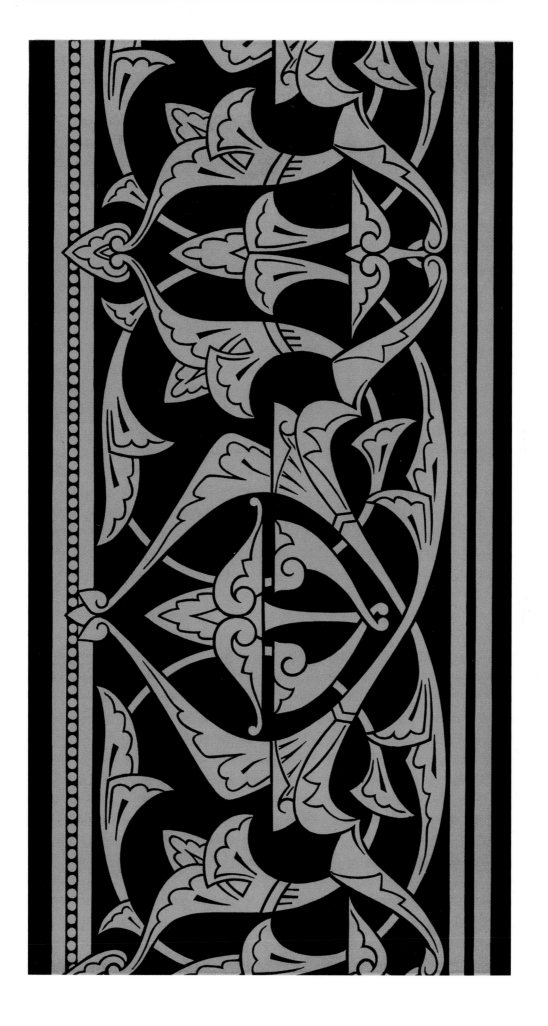

23

26

27

30

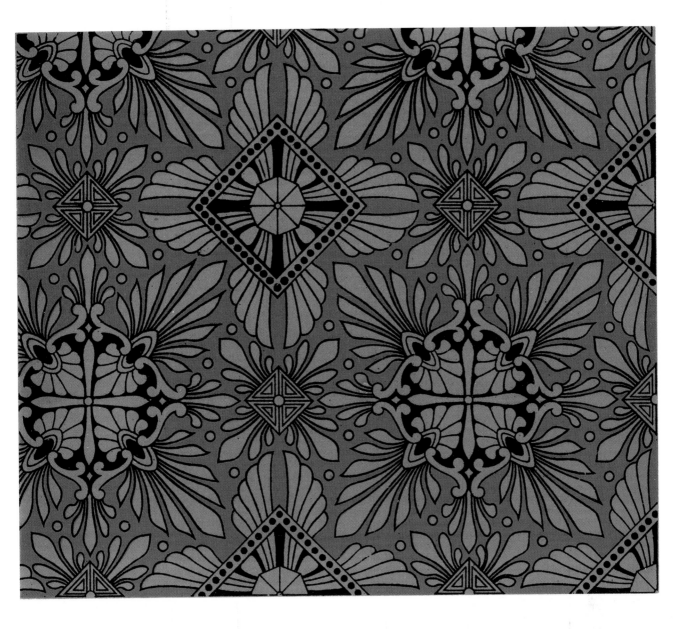

33

34

35

39

41

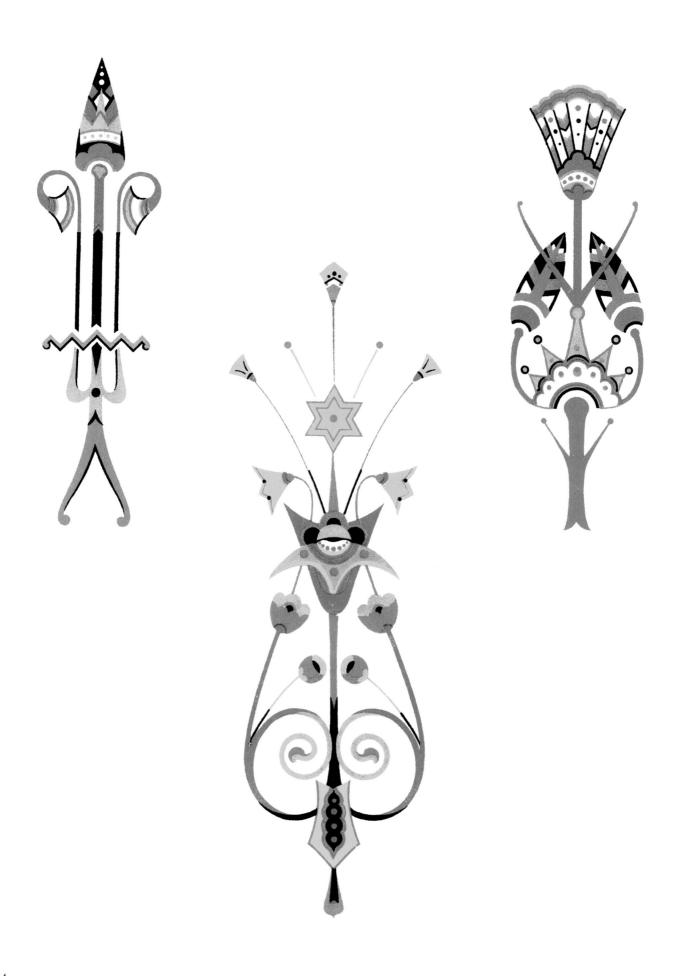

44

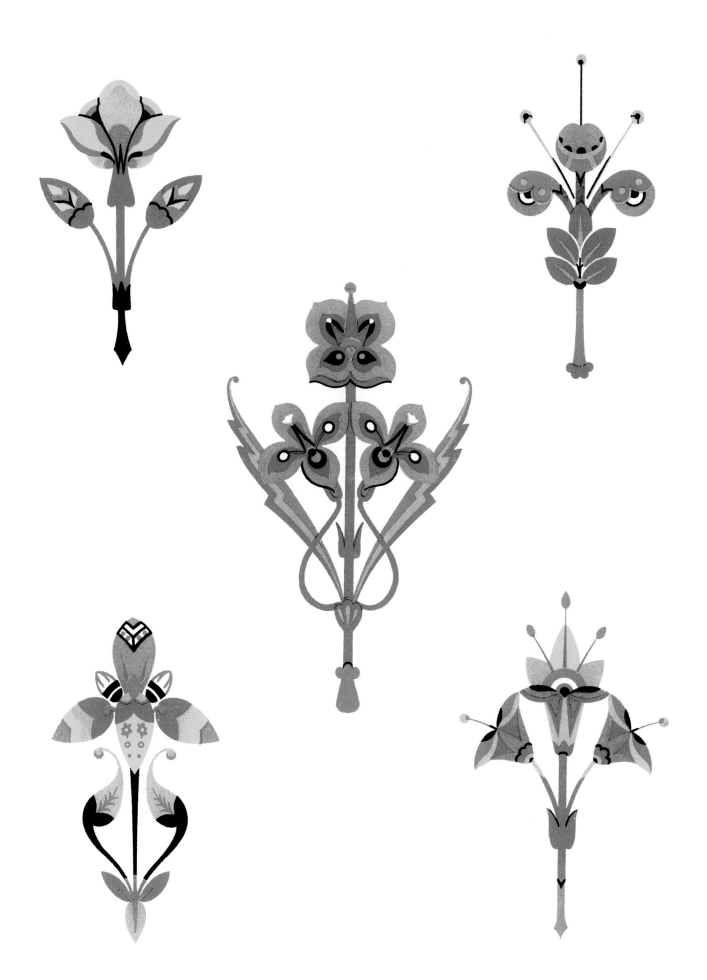

46

47

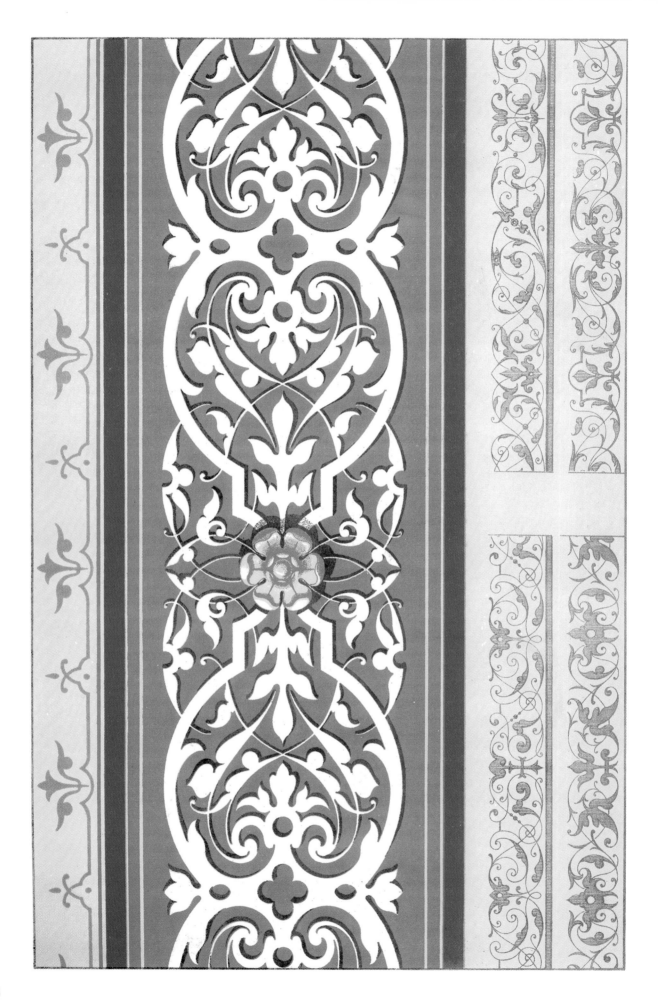

48

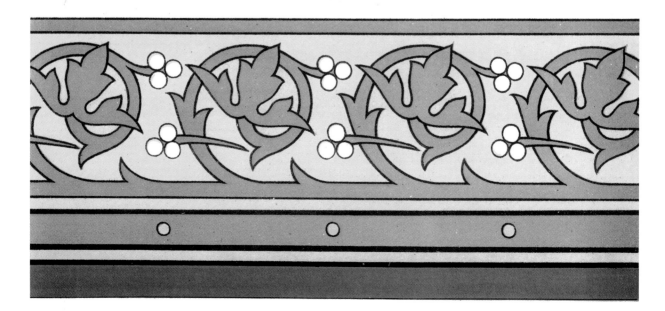

52

53

55

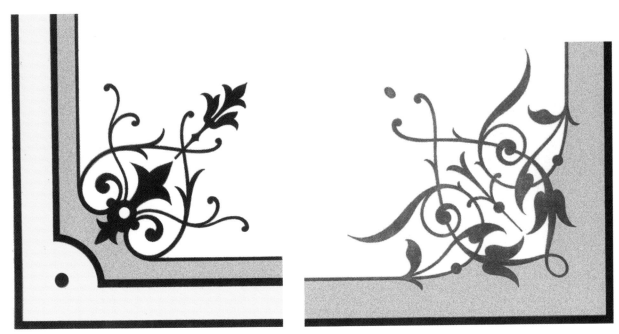

61

62

64

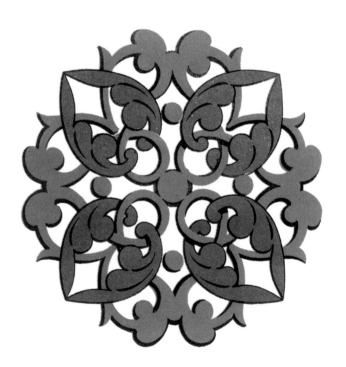

70

74